NINAIVIL

ANU

Copyright © Anu
All Rights Reserved.

This book has been published with all efforts taken to make the material error-free after the consent of the author. However, the author and the publisher do not assume and hereby disclaim any liability to any party for any loss, damage, or disruption caused by errors or omissions, whether such errors or omissions result from negligence, accident, or any other cause.

While every effort has been made to avoid any mistake or omission, this publication is being sold on the condition and understanding that neither the author nor the publishers or printers would be liable in any manner to any person by reason of any mistake or omission in this publication or for any action taken or omitted to be taken or advice rendered or accepted on the basis of this work. For any defect in printing or binding the publishers will be liable only to replace the defective copy by another copy of this work then available.

Dearest Sreenidhi,

Contents

Acknowledgements

Sculptor of this poet:

Mrs. AJ Lavanya

Gratitude:

Amma

Appa

Mr. Sabaridasan

Ms. Swathi K

Mr. Ajay Krishnan

Mr. Babu

Mrs. Priya

Ms. Kavitha

Mrs. Meenakshi

Mrs. Bhuvani

Ms. Gayathri

Ms. Sreenidhi

Mr. Meenakshi Sundaram

Initial Readers

Motivators

1. Ninaivil

Ra was roughly thirty.
Scripted with complete curiosity.
Ra had no heart and no heart.
Science was his only pumping part.
Hectic was life loaded with work.
For love, heart, people, went to lurk.
Ra worked with fascinating fissions.
He nailed at nuclear missions.
He created chain reactions.
His affairs were with atomic explosions.
Missiles flew to anywhere in the map
With his magical, but, scientifical snap.
It was the start of the two thousand
That bore a critical crisis in his land,
That launched long lines to get breads,
That stitched sufferings and designed deads.
Rich or poor, wise or fool, anyone, everyone
Had been hit hard and few were fully done.
Bankrupt Ra had money, too enough.
And was rich in lifeless, false, fancy stuff.
Ra was a dump of dust heap.
Gelled grime and dirt deep,

Blind on eyes and ripped of eyes,
Loose life was liable to become ice.
At walk, while return, with no mercy,
Ra shooed lovely asking vendors.
Hadn't felt to feed any parrot,
That knocked glass endlessly for grains.
Gave his face with fried with red,
To the lovely and playful butterfly.
Ra wasn't a rose, pink nor white.
People playing in his part were zero.
Life was lot and locked in his equations
To them, only, his emotions extended.
Heavily heavily engaged was he
Even in projects that fetched no fee.
Then took place a tragedy.
Everything of his, mastered mortality.
Ra had lost his ladylove, his work.
Cause was the country's crisis.
Salary for Ras was a noble dismay.
So he – a burden was briskly bowled away.
Tree standing nude,
Withered off leaves conclude,
Trees bend to weak and weak.
No more birdie's beauty beak,
Under the shades of saccharine.
The Tree stood saying what was vain.

ANU

Ra went mad without her,
Frying pans at glass.
Fellow, fell frightened, furious,
And performed pillow pierce.
Fists carved curves on floor,
And worn out went the door.
Ra spent all day at a corner,
Crying without her.
His hunger went to hide,
Ruined was Ra's bride!
Eyes stood strong and open
Red and weak with sleep broken.
Went switched as a street dog,
Went wiped out as waste.
At labs being chased,
And experiments decayed.
Ra wasn't given boots, not even one
Nor could he walk barefoot.
He and science had to, had to breakup!
Break his only, only coffee cup!
He was empty with facility,
To execute his own activity.
Ra felt mad at losing science,
Thus vanished his conscience.
He slowly started to freeze,
In the same bent were knees.
Heads down at the end,

Eyelids took a holiday.
Heartless heart stopped,
And eyeless eyes closed.
Fed up on frustrations,
And depressed on depressions.
No more could he,
With her everlasting memory.
Dispirited he made it instil:
That to give his, him a kill.
That was a very fine day.
Started by sunset and dismay.
Ra with rope entered room.
Sensibly something was to doom.
Set to rest the rotating fan.
And Ra chose to ban.
Rope was moulded to a noose,
Rightly placed were for its use.
He set foot over a chair,
And stood for an end there.
Sprang out a sonorous screech,
Then was there no no speech!
But! It was science that died!
Feels on fissions were tied,
Marking, the fan that went rest
To prevent papers' shuffled mess.
Penned papers in piles of piles
Were roped and given the last smiles.

The metal chair scratched tiles,
Ra climbed up to farewell files.
Opened was an old, too old, loft,
And those toxic thoughts went lost!
But, oh! opened loft opened a new way,
So, eyeless eyes, even they, made an eyeful display!
Eyes adorned elegant shiny wore,
And Ra's rocky bitter heart tore.
Tears slowly slid down,
For she stood in a pink gown!
Nostalgia for the memoryless!
Reminiscence for the past less!
A day - a moon sprang up
And both were up.
There she was; elegantly black,
Black in black,
Not short and not fat,
In her brown round spectacles.
A circle candy;
It had all started with that.
The duo dashed at her school,
Covered candy she dropped,
Tiny twelve, Ra, ran for it.
Ra gazed continuously at it.
Ra gazed at the rotating fan,
Thoughts on the forgotten ran.
It was an old photo of lost age,

A girl hugging Ra in teenage.
True love he had seen there,
But it was now nowhere.
"Ipo ethuku da alugira?
Ava yaru nu koda theriyala.
She stands a little older.
Probably any sister?
Ha! Amma appa veh theriyathu
Ithula unakku Akka kekutha?"
But, but! he cried, cried for someone!
Whose remembrance was none.
Ra had lost his memory,
Before his golden eighteen.
But, that history, mystery of past,
Had opened vessels in a bloodless heart.
Ra rolled and rolled over bed.
Night's sleep went dead.
Ra first saw some love.
He then went lively somehow.
Ra had true eyes born
And heartful heart went worn.
In dark, went oppressed to dormant.
Had that been, on light, left,
Sweating and struggling,
All day, all night.
How shall a seed – Ra, glow?
Once risen up to grow!

A colossal changeover was it:
Quickly came down roots
And shoot sprang up strong
To see light in life for first,
To dip, drench in brightness.
Woke the tiny shiny green!
The farmer went jolly happy.
The red farmer went happy.
To see her suppressed seed,
Into a set free, beauty green.
And so did the seed smile.
Ra was in ninth cloud's endless Nile.
Eager eyes yearned!
Heart craved for her!
Without her wraps of happy melt
His incompleteness was felt.
Now, it was his ideal transition,
To go back to her to awake.

A true fine day:
Ra, in park, called K, a far friend.
"Are you doing happy?
Are my motivations working?"
"K! I saw my past gem."
"What? Are you remembering them?"

The call seemed endless,
Ra finally went wordless,
On delivering her descriptions
K felt big burdens burnt away.
K's work of tuning him
Seemed having a huge shave.
"You don't even search
your mother,
kal nenjukaran,
But, intha
kathaya paaren!"
"Yes K. I don't even remember her."
"But my eyes, oh my eyes…
My eyes, unconsciously, collapsed."
"Some serious connection.
This is some true love.
This is so pure and true.
Strong sibling love Ra."
"Fine. Now, you are in track!"
K's obligations and Ra's stress pack
Seemingly slowly had a vanish.
"Your happiness is to replenish
"No more waste any day
Fly here to Bombay. Let us plan."
The sky was calm and blue.
A soothing breeze blew.
Autumn seemingly ended.

Spring visibly started.
Ra spun in the mid of all.
Mind went mad at love's call.
Ra booked a seat
To make life a repeat.
He was overseas
For the dense tall trees.
The plane landed on Mumbai.
Ra made a new way!
Streets were squeezed, overloaded.
Noise, not numerable, exploded.
"Gaadi. Gaadi. Gaadi!
Rukho! Madrasi"
Ra completely ignored the call
But the driver gave Ra a haul.
"Enge…poganu…Madrasi?"
Ra's understanding was less.
He gave dubieties a disregard
And gave K's address card
With the black-yellow car's call.
Ra set to crawl and crawl, only crawl.
Slow, only slow, he arrived.
K welcomed the tired,
Clock's spins spun,
And then came the famous bun.
The Vadapav was steaming,
With it, discussions developed a starting.

"Bun is nothing without pav
And so is you, Ra."
Threads of thoughts untied
And enlightenment went inside.
K strongly emphasised;
Immortality, with, is love devised!
Ra's narration on her, emanated.
"I'm extremely frustrated!"
Tired eyelids whenever fell,
Walked she with her lovely spell.
Ra saw flashing, flickering sights
He remembered moons and nights.
Love is who it is!
Love is who it is!
Love is the only everlasting,
Responsible for world's thriving.
It is, immortality and magic spilt.
Love makes lives together built.
Anywhere,
Nowhere,
Shall you be.
Love ties everyone.
Divine it is!
Perhaps, Almighty…is it?
K's strong advice was so.
To him, for her, to go.
"Even dad, before death, told that

Someone is waiting for you."
Then, sprinkled surmises stopped
"Search where?" – popped.
"Come on! We will find."
Interruptions entered behind.
Coats,
And boots,
Guns,
In target!
Bald head broke.
Sweat flushed, and it spoke!
K seemed heart attacked.
Visions seemed blacked.
Lips shivering!
Legs shaking!
A gunned gang peeked in!
Ra was in gunpoint's within.
"J knows, you are memory lost.
But, still, he wants you back, alive."
Cruel creature, J, was a minister
And had plans that were sinister.
A gunman - "Good one K!
Perfect acting for the pay."
Then, legs stood straight,
Lips sat calm and great.
Sweat vanished,
Drama banished!

Ra's motivation known,
K, went by money – blown.
Bags of notes, had kept the gunned.
Ra, upon the poet, went stunned.
Ruined was respect's magnitude,
That had arisen as gratitude.
Dear oh! Love wasn't love.
Money matters? How?
Notes unties the love knot.
Hard is where,
Cash is there.
But if, cash is in… in there!
But K's dad
Wasn't as bad.
Sabari he was,
A secular, peculiar, father.
A village's euphoria's cause.
This Ra' one and only and holy.
"But Ra, world stinks
But, her love never sinks."
Ra belittled,
Faith on one dwindled.
But on her love. No, not.
True love doesn't drought!
But oh! Then, Eyes whirled
Head swirled
Slowly fainted, faded.

Down lifeful as lifeless he lied.
Smiles K displayed,
For his Pav's devilry played.
They carried him to a station
To travel to an edge of the nation.
He was loaded into the train
Under the gunmen's campaign.
The train blasted.
Ra was transported.

Sneaking into the starting
of Ra's sixteens. Bleeding
he lied.
Soul dried.
She was his last sight.
Her skirt, circle cand… eyes went tight!
Soft and pulp fruit!
Sweet and cute flute!
Sugar fully in!
Jasmine!
How shall bouquet be crushed?
How shall infant be crushed?
She ran with a yelp
Crying for help.
Crossed and uncrossed,
Ran all to the church

For Sabari's search.
Then came the nearby white and white.
Ra was stitched here and there
Over the wear and tear.
And alas! He lied living dead
Without shaking head,
Breath in and breath out.
Silent was he throughout.
Sabari arrived after prayers
For all scares were menacing.
The white and white nodded,
Her family put down their head.
Coma – they declared.
Her eyes on tears were impaired.
Two white roses withered.
Loyal love shuttered.
Young immature hearts,
Lost each other's huge parts.
Breaths without oxygen,
Merciless was life in both even.
Cash to cure was high,
Hence was needed that fly.
Country Church was ready,
To fund the uncrossed.
She saved his circle candy
Keeping it as his memory.

Christ or science, someone.
But made him a souled one.
Although, as thorns stay in rose,
Seed inside soft pulp – grows,
Ra wasn't left without loss,
His memory had a full loss!
Ra went psychic after the wake,
To return – he didn't take.
Madness mixed, frustrations filled,
Silence, hatred, anger pilled,
Made his own away tent,
And only with science he went.
Ra fully forgot the past,
And never cared about it.
To Sabari, he lived paying gratitude
But still, he wasn't his everything.
For his Sabari's sake,
Few connects with K, did he make.

❧❧❧

Now, Ra was blacked.
Ra opened eyes, but was still blacked.
Pupils weren't diminished,
And still with black furnished.
Left right, hands he shook,
And, out of an apple basket, he stood.

The train was standing still,
Station was with silence's spill.
The gunmen weren't near,
Ra had been rid of any fear.
He set foot outside,
And gazed too wide.
Amidst the silent vibe,
Water dripped in a pipe.
Barefoot Ra headed to it,
For tap's assertable spit.
Still whirling, swirling, but, light,
Walked he, holding his head tight.
The water went splashed.
To light he went flashed!
The flickering flashes at dream,
Back it came with a gleam.
He remembered distorted dolls.
Many…A boy, an old one, a blue fly, so on.
Ra washed his face
And tried to trace
those meaningless meaningful
sights. Encoded it was. Beautiful!
Then, neither the puzzle broke
Nor the head broke!
A parrot interrupted the scene.
Wide, lively, large - Ra's eyes were seen.
The richness of red beak high,

And the shine of her tiny eye,
So she led him stammer.
Ra went flying behind her.
Ra had crossed platforms
Quick as storms.
The parrot was naughty.
Made him vigour less, the pie.
A greenery sneaked inside
Into a train faced a new direction.
Ra quickly got in
And made his chase a win.
The beauty flew to him
And stood on fingers, on him.
Love scenes took the play
And, suddenly, the parrot flew away.
The train started quickly,
Everyone were pushed lightly.
Of the shake, parrot departed.
But Ra… Ra, to a new place, started.
Ra neared the window there, there!
And progressed without knowing where.
Which train?
Where's train?
He didn't know.
But smiles did he show.
A seat, there he took,
With consciousness being overtook!

The train was set to Ooty.
Ra was totally mad.
In this search for his butterfly,
No map, no plan did survive.
Ra was mindless,
Unconscious.
Unconscious,
Mindless was Ra.
"En sogama iruka?"
Her feet would run to him,
Rises a sudden smile
On sounds of jingling anklets.
And sometimes,
Those magical eyes,
Were just enough
To light up the whole sky.
Darkness shall rule him, anywhere,
But it can't, if she is there.
Once, strain had mingled.
Eyes shrunk, forehead wrinkled,
Oh there! all actions froze.
An appealing look arose.
Balance down - slipped!
Eyes dripped and dripped.
Ra had frozen
Staring in sorrow
Over a stone, as a stone,

In the school park, as a statue.
His eyesight straight and sharp.
His lips withered and weathered
But, she was whiling with friends.
Was her face at the other,
Was her lips at the other,
World stories, house stories, all'd go
But eyes! They were finding Ra.
Her eyesight went to his eyes!
A smile she gives,
Miles high he goes.
Revived and restarted,
But, Mindless and unconscious.
But, mindless and unconscious
On mounting to bliss.
Hands and heart went stretched.
Legs circled and circled.
Dance and a kick he gave
And run among the orange trees
With white flowers,
With light feathers.
"I've to start thinking.
I've start finding.
Probably, where could she be?"
With nothing, stepped in he.
"She looks to be from Tamil Nadu.
I speak Tamil. Why not she be there?"

In Ra, too much strain mingled.
Eyes shrunk, forehead wrinkled,
Oh there! all actions froze.
An appealing look arose.
Balance down - slipped!
Eyes dripped and dripped.
Ra felt lost of track.
For he couldn't think the back.
For he tried and tried,
But only tried!
A big bitter rock wall – incessant,
Was built between buried past and present.
Ra had frozen
Staring in sorrow
Over a seat, as a stone,
In the Ooty train, as a statue.
His eyesight straight and sharp.
His lips withered and weathered.
Ended up in knowing nothing
On her beautiful sister.
Flushing tears did he show.
Head fell hopelessly on the window
Staring, on nothing, but, on her.
Parabola curved sharply down.
Outside were butterflies with friends,
One's face at the other,
One's lips at the other,

World stories, house stories, all'd go.
But one's eyes! They were finding Ra
Her eyesight came to his eyes!
Smileless, heartless, he went.
The train retarded and stopped.
Quickly returned the butterfly.
And Ra went styled shiny.
"You! You! Was it not you?.
In my thoughts. It was you!"
The fly was painted in blue
And sprinkled with black.
White curvy lines attached.
Green spots few to the final touch!
It reminded him, his past.
Reminded him, his past!
Ra ran between coaches.
The fly flew up and down.
He crossed many people;
Army uniforms,
Hanged with five strings,
And endless sounds springs.
Whitest white,
Whitish black,
Blackish white,
Blackest black,
He had crossed everyone.
And finally stood before one.

Then a smile she gave,
Miles high he went,
Revived and restarted.
But, Mindless and unconscious
But, mindless and unconscious
On mounting to too much bliss.
The fly stopped and landed.
And knots unravelled.
Unfolded went thrills and threats.
Was there the answer to questions,
Guide to the trek to her,
Mentor to that explorer.
Ra stood before a basket.
The basket was a greenery.
Ripe round mesmerising green,
About fourteen Jacks stood stacked.
Ra, uncontrolled, went to it.
But, he didn't remember any Jack.
But lied, "I love these."
But spoke facts, "She loves these."
An old woman – "Thambi!"
That soothing, soft, sweety,
Priceless word went spilled!
For it, fell Ra. He went pulled!
Ice turned and poured slowly.
"These fruits. This fly!
I have seen you."

"Me?" the Patti asked.
"You…" he paused.
"I think…I think… Oof!" he withered.
"I'm Dhi.
From Ooty.
I sell fruits in train
In various cities, various states.
Vaythu polapu la
Athaan alayanum."
A black faded stained lady;
Weak and wrinkly,
With a holed brown saree,
With a wore, tore bangle,
Thin and slim but big and pulp,
Sitting over the train floor.
"You speak English?"
"Very well."
"What do you want?
Seems you are stressed.
Patti can solve your mystery da.
What are you looking for?"
Ra was addicted!
She went to her love, afflicted.
He pulled the photo as a jet!
From his shirt pocket,
From his heart,
Standing there was them.

"I'm a memory loss person.
I don't have any relations.
But this girl. I'm searching for her.
I don't know her place,
her name,
or anything." - went he, lame.
"Goddess! Looks like Lakshmi."
"Aama la!"
"Oh God!
My girl she is!
I have seen her, in Ooty!
Take this fly – Ni. She'll guide you!"
Patti was in colour red?
A glowing figure, was she?
Slightly floating?
Tightly spelling?
A creature – red and divine?
Or a pseudo projection?
In that quaking train
Leading to love's domain,
Filled with fine and vain faces
With smooth, wrinkled and all cases.
Shall it be the summer's jasmine
Or the Jacks green, everything gets in.
Amid the rich filled lively vehicle
Stayed a soulful fading purple.
Ra was whiling near the window,

Going through the taste of air's flow.
Enlightening eyes and glowing heart
Ran reminiscing towards a restart.
Under shades of dark was time,
And the wheels were well in time.
Ra stretched legs and closed eyes.
Photo over his heart.
Picture in his dream.
Together they run! They play!
She and Ra revolved
Holding hands tight.
"Ring a Ring o roses!"
Shall he be tiny twelve
Or even up and tall thirteen,
But to her, was he young and young.
Little grown up was she.
But, shy, never she went!
For sake of miles in him
Could she do anything, everything.
"Pocket full of poises"
But oh! it had timed out then.
No more could he
With already existing strains.
No more could he, with her,
Was the most bothering.
He fell down,
Desperately, over the ground.

Two to twelve,
No day
Without strain's slay.
No day
Without cry's display.
Thigh strain told "How dare you escape?"
"How dare you escape?"
Interrupted was the sleep.
Those guns were back!
"J is calling you! Come!"
They whispered to their eyes, in fact.
Ra was still smiling dreaming.
The gunmen gave a good shake,
Ra flicked up in fright.
"Come" was an order
With guns shaking up and down.
Ra froze and was blank, dark, deep.
"Officers!" he screamed.
Army uniforms rushed with guns.
Gunmen split up as two and raced.
A quick chase commenced.
Ra sprang down
And gave his run.
An action sequence!
"The train mustn't stop!"
ordered Ra.
A gunman pulled the chain,

Brakes were applied.
Wheels screeched over the rails
The train stopped.
The gunmen jumped out.
Ra and two officers chased back.
Dark and deep it was aside.
An officer retarded and returned.
In the train, came a white-black, a bill.
Compromises were spoken.
"Is all in? All safe?" asked captain.
"Yes."
"Tomorrow is our big day. None to get lost."
"All safe captain."
Misleading, mistaken statements were they,
But mesmerizing statements were they.
Thirty minutes and more went.
Comprises were settled.
The train decided to take off.
The wheels overcame high friction,
Friction went less,
Then lesser.
The duo was almost lost.
He paused and planned to return.
They traced back to the train.
But their tracing was vain.
For no vehicle was there.
For it could have waited no more.

Their parabolas curved down.
Legs listlessly started walk.
"Pochu! Captain konuduvan!"
The young uniform cried.
"Tamil?"
"Yes!"
The walks extended.
By anxiety, were they apprehended.
Bent back and Ra put a pause.
On strain, down casted he was.
Of thighs, he was choked.
On strength, was he smoked.
No more could he
With already existing strains.
No more could he, to her,
Was the most bothering.
He fell down,
Desperately, over the ground.
She came to him
For him.
Her hands were enough
To trespass any tough.
A strong support - she stood so.
Thus to a haven did he go.
He came to him
To him.
His hands were enough

To trespass that tough.
A strong support - he stood so.
Thus to a haven did he go.
Aid did his shoulders sanction.
And Ra, calmy, made his progression.
But a decade did Ra go back.
To same feelings was he thrown back.
"Thank you" - a broken voice flowed.
In back, a short smile glowed.
Ra's fly still accompanied him.
His love never left him.
The fly fluttered over the other,
Dashed… dashed, at his name badge.
"Ni…Stop. Come back."
"Ni!"
The fly hovered on the officer.
Were knots to unravel?
Were thrills and threats to unfold?
There was; the real answer to questions.
Real guide to the trek.
Real mentor to that explorer.
"Where are you to?" – Officer.
"Probably" replied Ra "Ooty."
"Probably?"
"Yes. I am searching one."
"You are from?"
"Ooty only."

Ra's eyes enlarged.
Face bright,
Parabola up,
Quickly energy came.
A reviving power came.
Excited he was!
"Can you help me?"
He pulled that photo.
And stretched hands.
The fingers were just empty.
Photo had been slipped somewhere
A weight, a shadow got clipped there.
Thoughts of asking officer
about her ended in vain.
Sun probably was to set.
But, rather bounce back was what?
Ra quietly headed straight
And continued searching lights.
The nearby station came near,
The platform went visible.
Ni again dashed at his badge,
Ra, already upset, ignored.
"I think I have seen you."
"I too think I have seen you"
The duo got into the platform.
It was all quiet with just few.
The next train to Ooty

Wasn't even less sweety.
It was to shoot just after two days.
Young officer didn't have patience.
The duo travelled outside.
The midnight crowd was sparse.
There were still black-yellow cabs.
There were few cabs.
"Flights there? Ooty" – to the cabman.
"Coimbatore, in two hours."
The duo got in.
The car post-hasted to airport.
"Who are those gunmen?"
"J's people."
"J?"
"An evil minister."
The officer went silent.
Lips glued together.
And;
Eyes swirled,
Head ached,
Thoughts strained.
The airport grew bigger,
And the car stopped well nearer.
The officer who was starving,
Came aside from the fare.
Ra bore the expenses.
Ra - fading purple, drained.

The duo was silent.
Eye to eye.
Meaningless meaningful discussions went.
Officer broke shivering fear
And quickly pulled Ra's chain.
Feet then never touched ground.
Golden chain was perfect
To settle the flight fare.
For Ra was frozen, silent.
He was staring at his palm.
Ni had thrown something.
The badge - Officer's badge!
"Tejaa! Dei… Thambii!."
It was her real brother.
Ra got flashed on few past
On seeing the past.
Ra melted down as honey
in happiness and sweetness.
He chased him back
But ended in nothing.
He had already crossed limits.
Ra laughed to his eyes,
Ra calmly walked to the rail.
Poor rich he, made platform his bed.
Rich poor he, soared into the air.
"Don't I know any J?"
He learnt that known were they!

Questions arose - "Avan peru?"
"Ra…Ra." Dollar Ra dangled with the chain.
"J's chased son Ra? Aandavaa!"
"Akka is still waiting for this Ra?
Oh no! Epdi ivara viten?"
Tejas carved curves on laps
And slapped cheek tight.
He kept hands in chest and cried.
He then realised his missing badge.

J was a rich minister.
But, as a father - a sinister.
Overloaded with money,
But character wasn't any honey.
J wanted to win sympathy,
So could J win seats.
J thought to;
end his tiny son,
Write stories and win hearts,
Create his son dead of illness,
Make himself without heir,
Make himself deserving sympathy.
The tiny son got news.
He was just twelve.
Innocent he fell to J's legs
And promised to go out of sight.

He begged, cried, pleaded!
Merciless he, mercifully agreed.
Money played its part!
Love went apart!
Neither was the dad, wet
Nor the mom!
Orphaned he went,
Abandoned he left!
The ignorant tiny twelve,
Got into some bus,
Fare was his golden chain.
He got down somewhere,
And chased parrots, Jacks, flies, and more.
And somehow reached the Ooty convent.
There, turned life!
The helpless was given a hand.
He saw lovely eyes,
Heard caring words,
Felt secured.
"Unna thambi ah ninaichi solren..."
Ra had got a friend, a sister.
Her family accepted him.
He rose as their second son.
Ra's weeping towel
Or happiness recorder,
Anything, everything, was she.

A Chicken's slave,
And a curd'crave.
Different dialects,
Different towns,
Different people,
But a Sibling love!
Ra was fifteen
And the tragedy took place.
Ra was chasing her.
Young feets ran too fast.
For she had his circle candy.
Then oh! did limits go crossed.
The siblings reached away
To a too far road.
She was at an edge
And he was at another.
Crossed he without checks
A car then! A car was it!
How to narrate?
Oh! What words to use?
Soft and pulp fruit,
Sweet and cute flute,
Jasmine! Saccharine!
How shall a bouquet be crushed?
Young and fresh Ra
In the air
With a scary frozen sight

And spreadeagled body,
Dressed by blood
And kissed by pain.
Ra fell down on a bitter rock
And head had a severe knock.
She went drenched in fear.
In eyes, never did the sight expire.
It kept on haunting her.
It kept on haunting her ever!
She took the blame on her.
Guilt choked her.
Life turned pale and blur.
No more could she
With his lovely memory.
Eyeful eye paused, heartful heart stopped!
Until, a day, even that she
Remained quiet.
With smile forgotten
With energy vanished.
Her heart went passive.
Even that she, remained dumb.

Ooty Military Camp: That day:
Ra waited and only waited.
Badge went handed
And details were demanded.

ANU

A long file came,

And Teja's sheet went.

Address, contact and she – all with Ra.

Beauty truly bloomed back in him.

Bunches of white flowers

Stood straight and fresh.

Fragrance was too much

But best.

Ra was that Ra.

"Akka, aval anbin artham."

Words, divine, had the blossom.

White white rose which once went

Trekked tall tall terrains to tent

With wizardry or possibly divinity

Love let his life into eternal ecstasy

Ra – a fading purple,

a glowing white.

The restart in his hands.

The start in his hands.

Ra headed to unite.

Ra headed to live life.

There in Ooty, did he see

Her with redness as a sea.

The old wrinkled lady!

Stacking jacks did stand Dhi.

Dhi smiled at him!

Dhi smiled back at him!

The left sparse notes,
Went to Dhi, a butcher, a candyman,
The pure vegetarian packed meat
And the heartlful, childful bought candy
And bought round, round jacks.
Circle candy in hand, he went!
Ra went in shirt and trousers.
Trousers torn, reaching below knees.
Ra went with no beard, no moustache.
He went tiny, too tiny.
He went slim, so slim.
Ra went back, without any money.
Ra rang the bell.
She came running in her young feet.
She came in her brown shirt
In her white skirt
With her twin tails,
With her circle candy
The door was opened.
Tejas was understanding from the back.
She started to melt. Juicy eyes!
A fast run and a tight hug.
"Loosu!" the first word fell out.
"Akka!"
Tejas wiped eyes
And ran in joy.
A garland,

A framed photo,
They all went dissolved.
And life came back alive!
The same moon sprang up
And the same both were up.
There she was; elegantly black,
Black in black,
Not short and not fat,
In her brown round spectacles.
"This love, this care. How can I forget?"
"Mutaal" she broke in tears "You can't forget me."
Ra kept head over her laps.
She kept hand over hair and massaged.
"Pasikithu ka!"
Sight suddenly froze on hearing.
"I bought chicken for you."
Since the decade, never did she eat good.
She quickly ran to get a plate.
Her fingers mixed the rice,
And her fingers fed him.
"Even I didn't eat anything as good as this."
Understood he! Tejas peeped at the alone Ra,
For he was speaking to no one,
For he was eating no food,
Tejas, contentedly, let tears
And gave a great smile.
For his sweety went too happy.

If the parrot, she, Ni, Dhi.
Were his imaginations?
If this expedition,
Was his past's recreation?
If scenes of lost memory,
Were projected as hallucinations?
Then, then…Isn't love strong?
Immortal is love!
Magic is love!
Logicless is love!
Godly is love!
And, specially, is so, this white love!
Let;
Ra's life go hopeless,
Depressions make him mindless,
Yearning go extremely much,
Everything be forgotten.
But, his, love is wizardry! Perhaps, almighty?
Somehow, desires to get back
Happens, in reality,
If not, imagination.
But it happens!
It will! Whenever, wherever.
True love never ceases!
Love had dug the memory lost
And projected him the bliss.
How mad is a depression?

How mad is love?
Then, Ra spent life in happiness
With the flashing past in his present.
How shall love be forgotten?
How shall love forget one?
Shall be one dead
And one's moments dead.
But love is always alive!
But love is always in Ninaivil!
"Akka happy?" -
Tejas gazed at a star
And stared at the wise fool.
Tejas saw the star disappearing!
For she came back!
For she stood with Ra!
Days passed and
By a different typed love,
Ra got to unite with the other,
Tejas had offered him job.
However, Ra had rejected
And made life solely with her.
There were they!
Picking it again from
"Ring a Ring o Roses"
Circling in school uniforms!
Circling with school bags!
Thus were all moons, bright and full.

A candy it was!
That did start,
end and again start.
Sweetness did rejoice!
Born back by love, friends?,
siblings?, were Ra and Sre.

ANU

* 9 7 9 8 8 8 6 6 7 6 1 2 9 *